M
ACORNS!

by Inez Acevedo
illustrated by Eldon Doty

HOUGHTON MIFFLIN   BOSTON

Printed in China

ISBN 10: 0-618-89962-6
ISBN 13: 978-0-618-89962-3

789 0940 16 15 14 13

4500411354

"More acorns!" was the last thing Sanford Squirrel said to himself every night before he went to sleep. He said the same thing every morning as soon as he woke up.

Last year, Sanford collected 975 acorns before the cold days came. So far this year, he had 638 acorns. Sanford knew he needed more acorns—but how many more?

Read·Think·Write Do you think Sanford should estimate or calculate? Why?

One morning, Sanford's friend Alison came to visit.

"Hi Sanford," said Alison.

"More acorns!" replied Sanford. "I mean … Hi Alison."

"I can tell you're pretty busy," said Alison. "How many more acorns do you need?"

"I haven't figured that out yet," said Sanford. "I need 975 acorns. I know I have 638 so far, because I counted them. But how can I count the acorns I DON'T have?"

Read·Think·Write Should Sanford add or subtract to find how many more acorns he needs?

5

"Well," said Alison, "you could subtract to find out how many more you need."

"SUBTRACT?" exclaimed Sanford. "Galloping oak trees, Alison! I don't want to TAKE AWAY acorns, I want MORE acorns!"

"Yes, Sanford, I get it," replied Alison. "But subtracting isn't always about taking away. Sometimes you subtract when you know how many are in one part of a group, and you want to figure out how many are in the other part.

"You want 975 acorns, right? You have 638, so you need to find out how many are in the part of the group you DON'T have."

Read·Think·Write What numbers should Sanford subtract to find out how many more acorns he needs?

"Hmmm," said Sanford thoughtfully. "I could draw place-value blocks to help me subtract!"

"Or I could write the subtraction on paper and check my answer by estimating."

And Sanford did just that.

Read·Think·Write Estimate the number of acorns Sanford still needs to collect.

"Well I won't find more acorns inside this house!" said Sanford. "I'd better go outside and get to work!"

"Hurray!" exclaimed Sanford. "More acorns!"
Then he paused. "More acorns! That means I'll
have to figure it out all over again!"

1. Use one of Sanford's ideas to figure out how many acorns Sanford still needs to collect. How close was your calculated answer to your estimate?

2. The next day, Sanford collected 78 acorns outside his house. How many more acorns does he still need to find?

3. When might you decide to estimate instead of calculating?

Activity

Predict/Infer If you had a collection, what would you collect? Tell how many there are in your collection now (more than 100), and how many there will be when the collection is done (less than 1,000). Estimate how many more you need, and then show two different ways to calculate it.